BUILDING BIG
ANCIENT
ARCHITECTURE

by Joyce Markovics

 CHERRY LAKE PRESS
cherrylakepublishing.com

Published in the United States of America by Cherry Lake Publishing Group
Ann Arbor, Michigan
www.cherrylakepublishing.com

Reading Adviser: Beth Walker Gambro, MS, Ed., Reading Consultant, Yorkville, IL
Content Adviser: Jeffrey Shumaker, AICP, Urban Designer, Planner, Architect, and Educator
Book Designer: Ed Morgan

Photo Credits: freepik.com, cover; freepik.com, title page; unsplash.com/Sam Moghadam Khamseh, 4–5; Wikimedia Commons, 5 inset; Wikimedia Commons, 6 top; Wikimedia Commons, 6 bottom; Public Domain, 7; Wikimedia Commons/Kaufingdude, 8; © Luxon Portfolio/Shutterstock, 9; freepik.com, 10–11; freepik.com, 12; unsplash.com/Ibrahim Rifaith, 13; freepik.com, 14–15; freepik.com, 16; freepik.com, 17; unsplash.com/shark ovski, 18–19; unsplash.com/Ameena Tasneem, 20 top; Wikimedia Commons/Ptolemy Thiên Phúc, 20 bottom; unsplash.com/avinash uppuluri, 21; freepik.com, 22; unsplash.com/Alex Azabache, 23; freepik.com, 24–25; Wikimedia Commons, 25; freepik.com, 26–27.

Cherry Lake Press is an imprint of Cherry Lake Publishing Group.

Library of Congress Cataloging-in-Publication Data

Names: Markovics, Joyce L., author.
Title: Ancient architecture / Joyce Markovics.
Description: Ann Arbor, Michigan : Cherry Lake Publishing, 2023. | Series:
   Building big : amazing architecture | Includes bibliographical
   references and index. | Audience: Grades 4–6
Identifiers: LCCN 2022039520 (print) | LCCN 2022039521 (ebook) | ISBN
   9781668919811 (hardcover) | ISBN 9781668920831 (paperback) | ISBN
   9781668923498 (adobe pdf) | ISBN 9781668922163 (ebook) | ISBN
   9781668924822 (kindle edition) | ISBN 9781668926154 (epub)
Subjects: LCSH: Architecture, Ancient—Juvenile literature.
Classification: LCC NA210 .M37 2023 (print) | LCC NA210 (ebook) | DDC
   722—dc23/eng/20220822
LC record available at https://lccn.loc.gov/2022039520
LC ebook record available at https://lccn.loc.gov/2022039521

Printed in the United States of America
Corporate Graphics

CONTENTS

"House of the Mountain"

Rising out of the desert in southern Iraq is a spectacular sight. It's an ancient four-sided pyramid called a ziggurat (ZIG-oo-rat) that dates from 2100 BCE. That's nearly 4,000 years ago! King Ur-Nammu built the striking structure as a **temple** for a moon goddess called Nanna. The ziggurat was originally about 69 feet (21 meters) tall and 213 feet (65 m) wide. At that height, people would have seen it from miles away. The ziggurat would have served as a symbol of the king's power and wealth.

When it was built, the Ziggurat of Ur had three distinct layers, or steps, with a temple on top. Workers constructed the core using mud bricks and the exterior from sunbaked bricks, some of which were painted white and black. The temple was decorated with **vibrant** glazed blue tiles. Long ago, people believed that gods and goddesses lived in their temples. So, the temple would have had a bedroom where Nanna could sleep. There would have also been a kitchen where a human servant could prepare food for the goddess.

Pictured is the Ziggurat of Ur. The word *ziggurat* comes from a Babylonian word meaning "house of the mountain." Babylon was a huge city in Mesopotamia, an ancient region of present-day Iraq.

This image shows what the ziggurat may have originally looked like.

The Great Temple at Múgeyer, from the west.

A sketch of the discovery of the Ziggurat of Ur

Over the centuries, parts of the Ziggurat of Ur crumbled into ruins. It was rebuilt around 500 BCE. After that, the structure once again fell into disrepair. In 1850, a British **archaeologist** named William Loftus saw a huge, irregularly shaped mound in the Iraqi Desert. Could it be an ancient building, he wondered? Loftus called for the area to be **excavated**. Slowly, over the course of many decades, the ruins were uncovered.

Archaeologist and explorer
William Loftus

But only the ziggurat's **foundation** was intact. In the 1920s, husband and wife archaeologists Leonard and Katharine Woolley completed the excavations, revealing the ziggurat and three grand staircases. Leonard Woolley called it "the most **imposing** of the ancient **monuments** of Iraq." The Woolleys also found incredible architectural details, including drains called "weeper holes" that carried water away from the building during heavy rains. They also discovered small **niches** in the exterior walls that helped keep the interior section cool.

This photo shows one of the ziggurat's partially excavated staircases.

Each brick used to build the ziggurat weighed as much as 33 pounds (15 kilograms) and had the king's stamp on it. More than 720,000 bricks were needed to build the first step of the structure! Over the centuries, local people took some of the bricks for their own building projects.

The ziggurat restoration in the 1980s

In the 1980s, the Iraqi government **restored** a portion of the Ziggurat of Ur. They repaired and rebuilt the **façade** of the lower step. They also restored the three giant staircases. Archeologists who studied the building believe that the sloping sides and steps may have been covered with lush gardens when the ziggurat was originally constructed.

FACT BOX

An architect is a person who designs buildings. Architecture is the art of designing buildings.

Ziggurats are some of the world's oldest surviving buildings. They show the skill of the ancient architects who designed them. Many ziggurats were built throughout ancient Mesopotamia. Twenty-five are known. The largest ziggurat is in southwestern Iran and is 80 feet (24 m) high, although it is thought to be less than half of its original size. The Ziggurat of Ur, however, is the best-**preserved**. This stunning monument is one of many types of ancient architecture that can be found around the world!

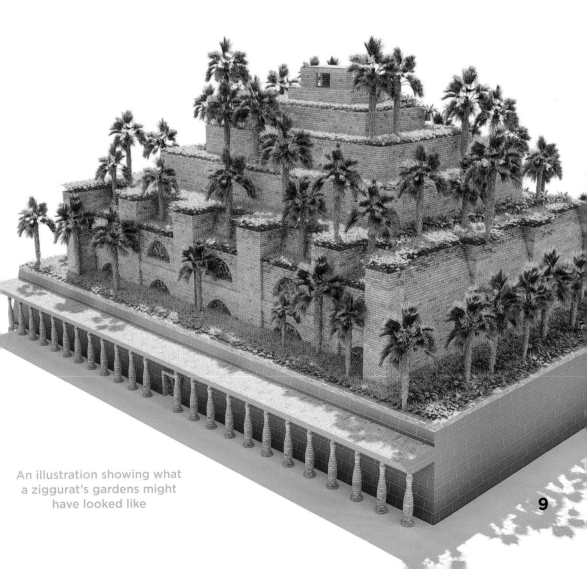

An illustration showing what a ziggurat's gardens might have looked like

What Is Ancient Architecture?

Ancient means belonging to the distant past. So ancient architecture includes buildings and structures, such as walls and bridges, that were built long ago by early **civilizations**. The earliest examples of architecture came from **prehistoric** people. They built huts from **mammoth** bones, small islands called crannogs, and stone houses, for example. When these early people switched from hunting and gathering their food to farming, they established larger and more permanent communities. These communities grew into civilizations that gave rise to the first cities. More advanced architecture and lasting buildings then followed.

There was a wide variety of ancient buildings and structures, and each had a different use. For example, the ancient Egyptians built pyramids as tombs to house their dead. In Asia, early people assembled the Great Wall of China to protect themselves against enemy invaders. And the Mayan people of Central America constructed temples to worship their gods.

FACT BOX

The Great Wall of China was built over hundreds of years by Chinese emperors to keep their lands safe. The oldest parts date to 221 BCE. It's one of the largest human-made structures ever built.

The Great Wall of China

Architecture is not just about function. It's also about form, or the way something looks. Every ancient culture introduced its own artistry and style of architecture. Some of the structures early architects designed were grand and impressive. They included a lot of decoration, such as intricately carved **reliefs** or columns. Others were plain and **unadorned**, made from blocks of stone or bricks.

An early stone column beautifully decorated with a creature called a griffin in Persepolis, Iran

Whether grand or simple, every structure required a lot of skill to design and build. However, in ancient times, people did not have computers, power tools, and big machines like cranes and bulldozers as we do today. They had very simple tools. Yet they still managed to design and build incredible things. They carved great palaces out of solid rock and created magnificent stadiums and theaters that held thousands of people. These early architects also built entire cities. The process was often slow, but their methods worked, which is why so many of the structures are still standing today.

Ancient steps in India leading to an area that was used to hold water

Experts call the places in which people live and work the "built environment." The earliest built environments date back thousands of years!

Ancient Egypt

The ancient Egyptians were some of the greatest ancient architects. Ancient Egypt was one of the first civilizations in the world. It began about 6,000 years ago in northern Africa. The ancient Egyptians are best known for their towering pyramids. But they also built many other structures, such as houses, palaces, tombs, and temples. Their architecture featured big stone elements, such as sloping walls, giant statues, and columns that looked like papyrus and other plants.

FACT BOX

Other ancient cultures built pyramids of their own. These include the Nubian people of Africa, the Chavin people of South America, and the Mayan people of Central America.

The oldest Egyptian pyramid is Djoser's Step Pyramid at Saqqara, dating from 2550 BCE. It was built by an architect called Imhotep as a tomb for King Djoser (or Zoser). This pyramid is the first known large-scale stone structure ever built! Imhotep figured out how to move large stone blocks using sleds, rollers, and ramps. He layered the stones on top of each other. When completed, the pyramid was 204 feet (62 m) tall. It originally had columns that looked like bundled papyrus reeds and blossoms. The pharaoh's actual tomb was located 92 feet (28 m) under the pyramid. To reach it, a person would have to walk through a maze of hallways covered with brightly painted artwork.

Djoser's Step Pyramid is made from white limestone and granite.

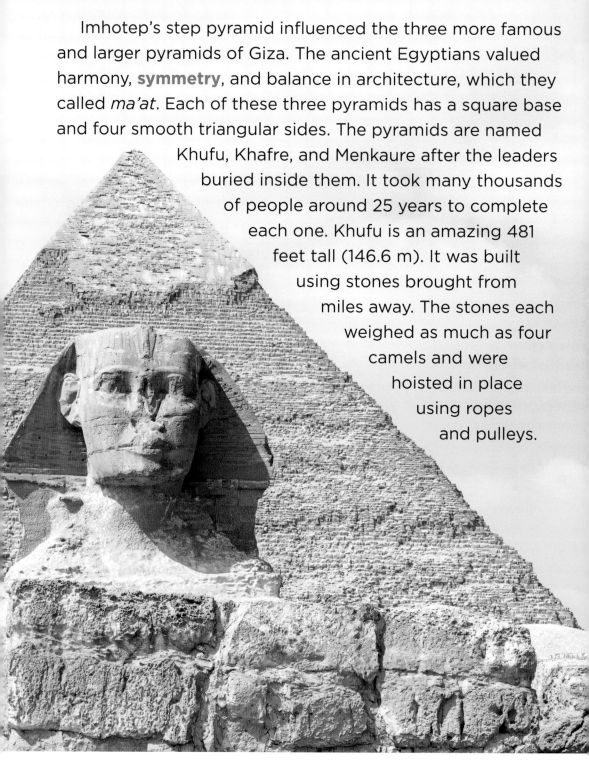

Imhotep's step pyramid influenced the three more famous and larger pyramids of Giza. The ancient Egyptians valued harmony, **symmetry**, and balance in architecture, which they called *ma'at*. Each of these three pyramids has a square base and four smooth triangular sides. The pyramids are named Khufu, Khafre, and Menkaure after the leaders buried inside them. It took many thousands of people around 25 years to complete each one. Khufu is an amazing 481 feet tall (146.6 m). It was built using stones brought from miles away. The stones each weighed as much as four camels and were hoisted in place using ropes and pulleys.

A sphinx statue with the head of a pharaoh and the body of a lion stands near the pyramids of Giza.

In addition to the great pyramids, the ancient Egyptians built impressive temples. An outstanding example was designed for a female king named Hatshepsut. It was dug into solid rock and has three terraces wrapped with **colonnades**. Ramps lead to the terraces, and carvings of Hatshepsut cover the temple. It is one of many magnificent buildings showcasing ancient Egyptian design and **ingenuity**.

The Temple of Hatshepsut

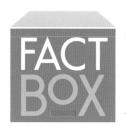

FACT BOX

The ancient Egyptians also built simpler structures. They invented molds to make mud and straw bricks for building homes.

Architecture
Around the World

In other parts of the ancient world, different styles of architecture developed. Thousands of years ago, the people of China built temples and houses made from wood topped with glazed tiles. The corners of the roofs gracefully curved upward. Many of these structures were built on raised platforms. Often, buildings were clustered around a courtyard. The outsides of the buildings were painted using deep red, green, and yellow. Inspired by nature, the Chinese prized harmony and order in their designs.

The highly decorated roof of an early Chinese building

FACT BOX

German architect Ludwig Mies van der Rohe (1886–1969) said architecture began when "two bricks were put together well."

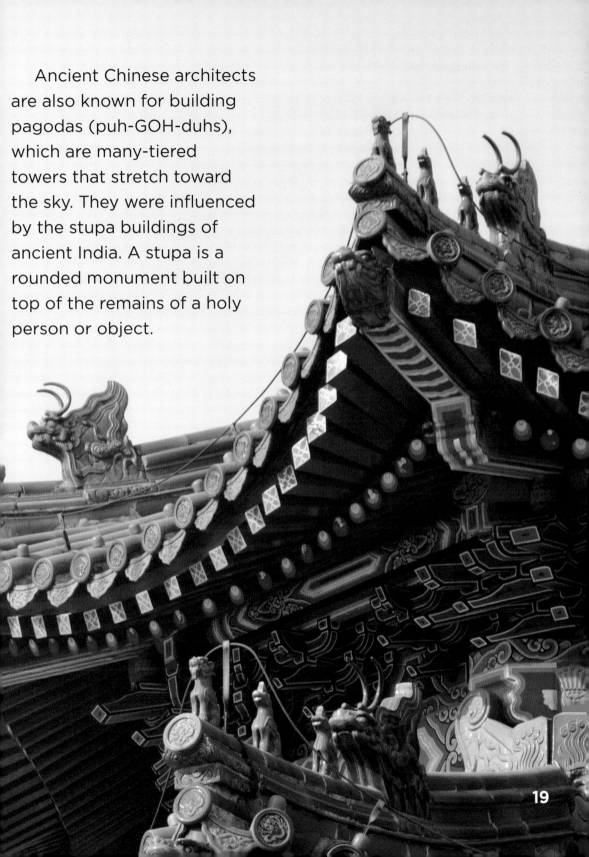

Ancient Chinese architects are also known for building pagodas (puh-GOH-duhs), which are many-tiered towers that stretch toward the sky. They were influenced by the stupa buildings of ancient India. A stupa is a rounded monument built on top of the remains of a holy person or object.

One of the oldest stupas in India

Ancient India had its own style of architecture, which **evolved** over time. At first, there were simple rock shrines cut into caves. Then more than 2,000 years ago, an emperor named Asoka built a group of stupas in honor of the Buddha. The religion of Buddhism is based on the teachings of the Buddha. The domed Buddhist stupas are some of the oldest stone structures in India. Asoka also constructed polished stone pillars near the stupas that featured finely carved animals, such as lions and geese.

One of the lion columns

After Asoka's stupas came larger and more elaborate Hindu temples. They featured huge gates and arched windows and doors. Some were decorated with hundreds or thousands of sculptures of Hindu gods, animals, people, flowers, or scenes. The temples had soaring pyramid-shaped towers called *shikhara*, where Hindus believed heaven and Earth met. They thought the temples were sacred places where gods and people were brought together.

An ancient Hindu temple

21

Greek and Roman

In the western part of the world, the ancient Greeks produced a uniquely Greek form of architecture. Though they did not invent columns, they created three main styles, or orders, of columns. These are Doric, Ionic, and Corinthian. Each column type has a special design, known as a capital, on the top. Doric capitals are plain. Ionic capitals look like a scroll. And Corinthian capitals have lots of **acanthus** leaves as decoration. The ancient Greeks built temples and other buildings using these various columns. Most Greek temples also had a porch called a portico and a rectangular foundation. Marble was used as the main building material. One of the most celebrated examples of ancient Greek architecture sits on a hill in Athens, Greece. Called the Parthenon, it's a marble temple made with Doric columns. Since that time, the ancient Greeks have had a huge impact on the architecture of the rest of the world.

Doric   Corinthian   Ionic

The ancient Romans came after the Greeks. They were heavily influenced by the Greeks but also made their own contributions to architecture. One important Roman invention was concrete—a mix of sand, water, and gravel. Roman architects used concrete to build strong, thick walls quickly. In addition, they used concrete to make perfectly smooth areas on curved surfaces, such as domes.

The Colosseum was designed to hold 50,000 to 80,000 people! Visitors watched men called gladiators fight wild animals or other men in the arena.

The Romans were also known for building big public buildings. In 70 CE, a Roman emperor named Vespasian constructed an enormous stadium. Built using rock and concrete, it's known as the Colosseum and is still standing today! Another notable ancient Roman structure is the Pont du Gard **aqueduct** in France from 15 CE.

Artwork showing Vitruvius presenting a plan to the Roman Emperor Augustus

Vitruvius was an important Roman architect and engineer. He wrote a multi-volume book about architecture that focused on three principles—strength, functionality, and beauty.

Lasting Contributions

For thousands of years, humans have been designing places where they can live, work, and worship. However, only a small number of ancient buildings have survived. Many were **eroded** by wind and rain over the centuries or destroyed by people. Despite this, the ancient architecture that remains continues to have a lasting effect. The history of architecture is the story of people. It helps modern people learn about past civilizations and cultures. And it also impacts today's architecture.

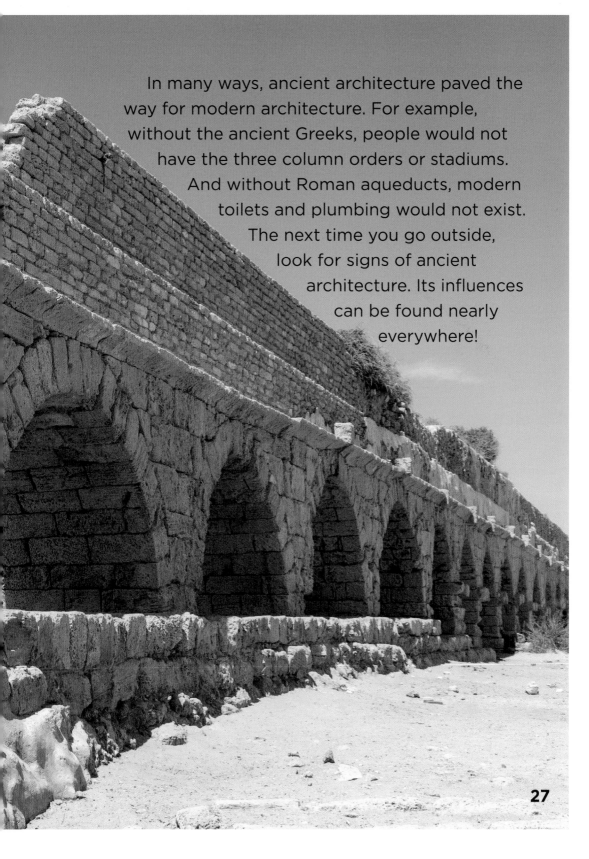

In many ways, ancient architecture paved the way for modern architecture. For example, without the ancient Greeks, people would not have the three column orders or stadiums. And without Roman aqueducts, modern toilets and plumbing would not exist. The next time you go outside, look for signs of ancient architecture. Its influences can be found nearly everywhere!

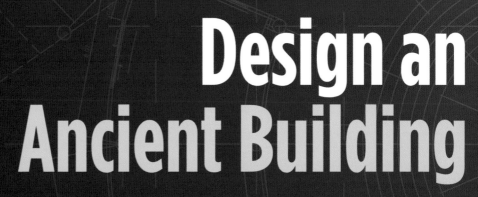

Design an
Ancient Building

Think about what you just learned about ancient
architecture in this book. Now use that information
to design your own ancient building!

DESIGN CONCEPT: What is your idea for your building? Where will it be located? What will it be used for? What materials will you use to build it? Consider your building's form *and* function.

PLAN: Think about what the exterior and interior of your building will look like. How will people move around and through your building? How will it fit into the landscape? How big or small will it be?

DRAW: Grab some paper and a pencil. Sketch the floor plan of your building to show the arrangement of rooms. Label each room. Next, draw the exterior, noting what materials will be used.

BUILD A MODEL: Use materials around your home, such as pebbles, paper, cardboard, scissors, straws, popsicle sticks, and glue, to build a small model of your building.

REFINE YOUR PLAN: What works about your design? What doesn't work? Make any needed changes to improve your building.

GLOSSARY

acanthus (uh-KAN-thus) resembling the leaves of a plant that has spiny leaves

aqueduct (AK-wih-duhkt) a channel for holding and carrying water

archaeologist (ar-kee-OL-uh-jist) a scientist who learns about ancient times by studying old buildings, tools, and other things

civilizations (siv-uh-luh-ZEY-shuhnz) the society, cultures, and ways of life of particular areas

colonnades (kol-uh-NEYDS) a series of regularly spaced columns

eroded (ih-ROHD-uhd) worn away

evolved (ih-VOLVD) developed over time

excavated (EKS-kuh-vay-tid) uncovered by digging

façade (fuh-SAHD) the front of a building that's usually decorative

foundation (foun-DAY-shuhn) a solid structure on which a building is built

Hindu (HIN-doo) relating to the religion of Hinduism in South Asia, which involves the worship of many gods

imposing (im-POZ-ing) stately and impressive

ingenuity (in-juh-NOO-ih-tee) being clever and resourceful

mammoth (MAM-uhth) a large kind of elephant that died out long ago

monuments (MON-yuh-muhnts) buildings other structures built to honor a famous person or event

niches (NEESH-uhs) small, shallow spaces

prehistoric (pree-hi-STOR-ik) before the time when people began to reco history

preserved (pri-ZURVD) kept in good condition

reliefs (rih-LEEFS) sculptures that are carved, molded, or stamped so as to stand out from the surface

restored (ri-STORD) returned to its original condition

sacred (SAY-krid) holy; religious

symmetry (SIM-ih-tree) the quality of being made up of exactly similar parts facing each other

temple (TEM-puhl) a building used for worship

unadorned (un-UH-dawrned) not decorated; plain

vibrant (VAHY-bruhnt) bright and striking

READ MORE

Allen, Peter. *Atlas of Amazing Architecture*. London: Cicada Books, 2021.

Armstrong, Simon. *Cool Architecture*. London: Pavilion, 2015.

Dillon, Patrick. *The Story of Buildings*. Somerville, MA: Candlewick Press, 2014.

Glancey, Jonathan. *Architecture: A Visual History*. London: DK, 2021.

Moreno, Mark. *Architecture for Kids*. Emeryville, VA: Rockridge Press, 2021.

LEARN MORE ONLINE

Architecture for Children
https://archforkids.com

Britannica Kids: Architecture
https://kids.britannica.com/students/article/architecture/272939

Center for Architecture: Architecture at Home Resources
https://www.centerforarchitecture.org/k-12/resources/

Lego Design Challenge
https://www.architects.org/uploads/BSA_LWW_LEGO_Challenge.pdf

STEAM Exercises: Kid Architecture
http://www.vancebm.com/kidArchitect/pages/steamExercises.html

INDEX

ABOUT THE AUTHOR

Joyce Markovics has written hundreds of books for young readers. She lives in a nearly 200-year-old carpenter Gothic style house along the Hudson River. Joyce would like to thank architect, designer, and city planner Jeff Shumaker for his insight and help creating this series.